FLASHCARD BOOKS

NUMBERS
SHAPES & COLORS

ENGLISH
to
GERMAN

FLASHCARD BOOK

BLACK & WHITE EDITION

HOW TO USE:

• READ THE ENGLISH WORD ON THE FIRST PAGE.

• IF YOU KNOW THE TRANSLATION SAY IT OUT LOUD.

• TURN THE PAGE AND SEE IF YOU GOT IT RIGHT.

• IF YOU GUESSED CORRECTLY, WELL DONE!
IF NOT, TRY READING THE WORD USING THE PHONETIC PRONUNCIATION GUIDE.

• NOW TRY THE NEXT PAGE.
THE MORE YOU PRACTICE THE BETTER YOU WILL GET!

BOOKS IN THIS SERIES:
ANIMALS
NUMBERS SHAPES AND COLORS
HOUSEHOLD ITEMS
CLOTHES

ALSO AVAILABLE IN OTHER LANGUAGES INCLUDING:

FRENCH, GERMAN, SPANISH, ITALIAN,

RUSSIAN, CHINESE, JAPANESE AND MORE.

WWW.FLASHCARDEBOOKS.COM

One

Eins

Ai-ns

Two

Zwei

Zw-ai

Three

Drei

Dry

Four

Vier

Fear

Five

Fünf

Fue-nf

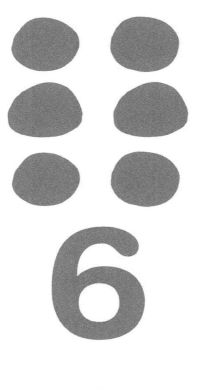

6

Six

Sechs

Sex

Seven

Sieben

See-ben

Eight

Acht

Ah-cht

Nine

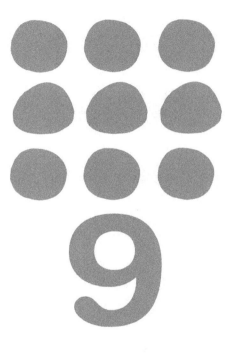

Neun

Neu-n

Ten

Zehn

Tze-hn

Eleven

Elf

Elf

Twelve

Zwölf

Zwoe-lf

Thirteen

Dreizehn

Dry-zeh-n

Fourteen

Vierzehn

Fear-zeh-n

Fifteen

Fünfzehn

Fue-nf-zeh-n

Sixteen

Sechzehn

Sex-zeh-n

Seventeen

Siebzehn

Seeb-zeh-n

Eighteen

Achtzehn

Ah-cht-zeh-n

19

Nineteen

Neunzehn

Neu-n-zeh-n

20

Twenty

20

Zwanzig

Tz-fun-zig

30

Thirty

30

Dreißig

Dry-zig

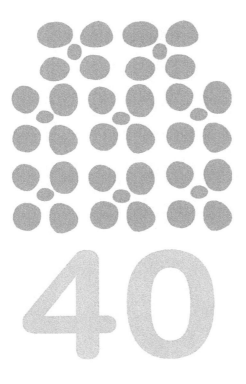

40

Forty

Vierzig

Feat-zig

50

Fifty

50

Fünfzig

Fue-nf-zig

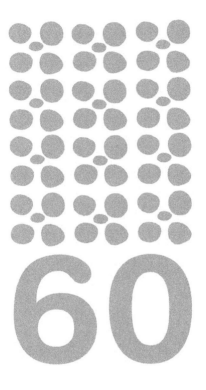

60

Sixty

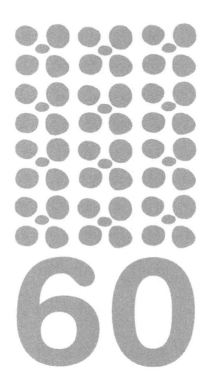

60

Sechzig

Sex-zig

70

Seventy

70

Siebzig

Seeb-zig

Eighty

80

Achtzig

Ah-cht-zig

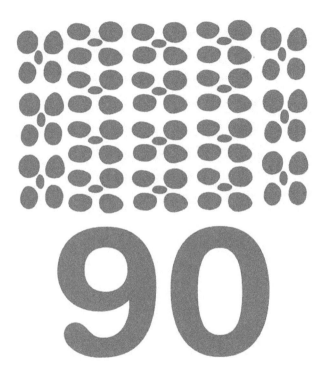

90

Ninety

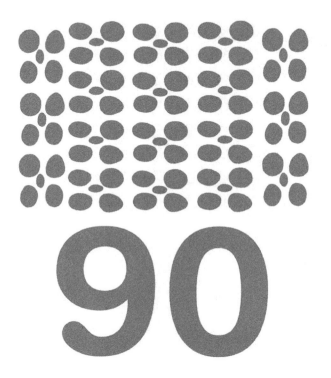

90

Neunzig

Neu-n-zig

One Hundred

Einhundert

Ai-n-hun-dert

One Thousand

Eintausend

Ai-n-tau-send

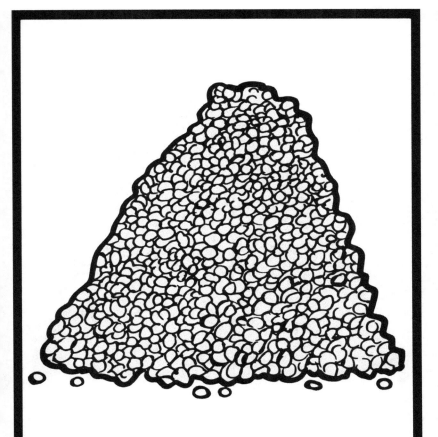

One Million

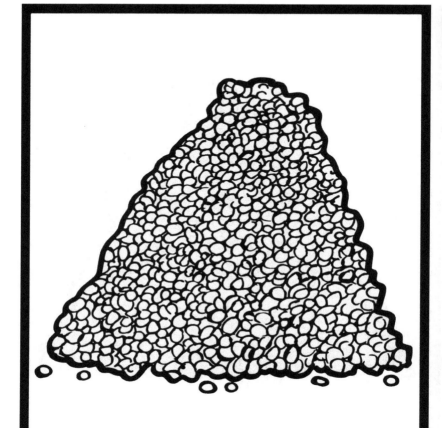

Eine Million

Ai-neh Mill-ion

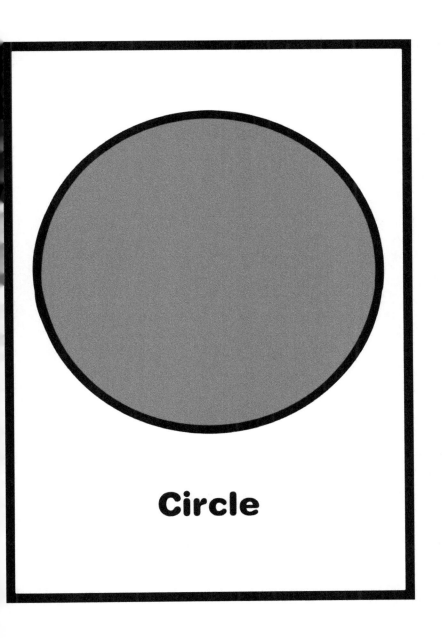

Circle

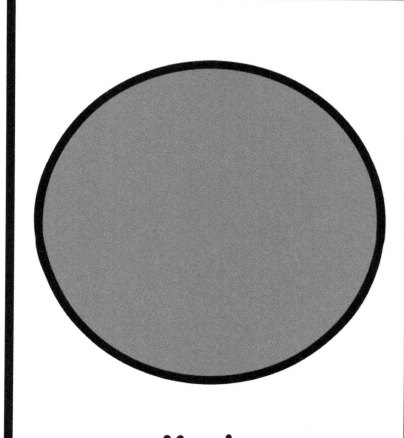

Kreis

Cry-s

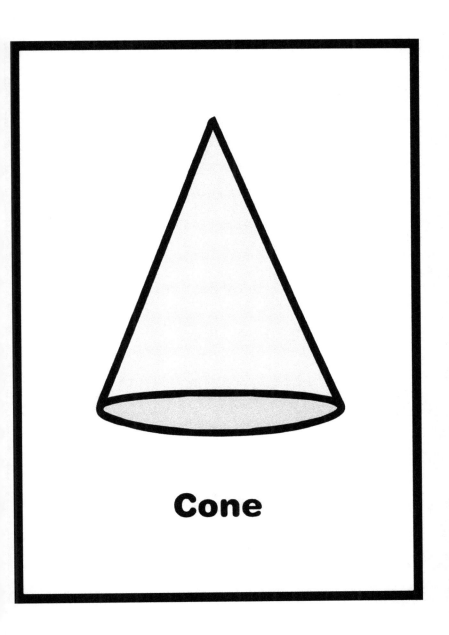

Cone

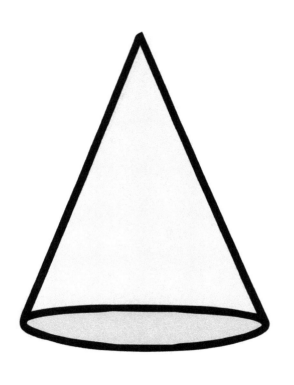

Kegel

Ke-ge-hl

Crescent

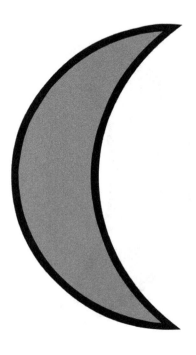

Halbmond

H-alb-mon-d

Cube

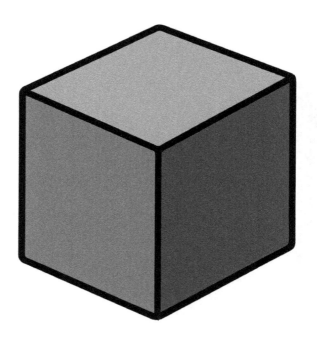

Würfel

Wuer-fell

Cylinder

Zylinder

Clyinder

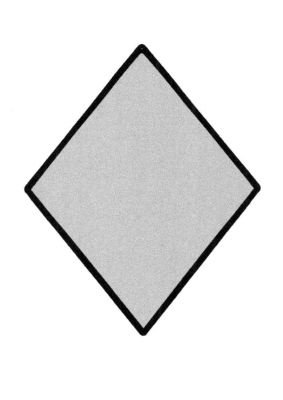

Diamond

Diamant

Dee-a-mant

Heart

Herz

Hertz

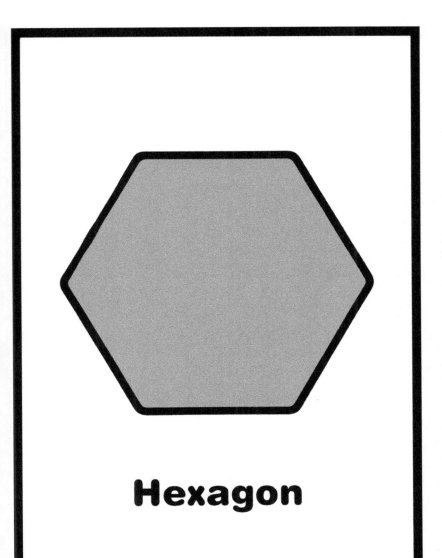

Hexagon

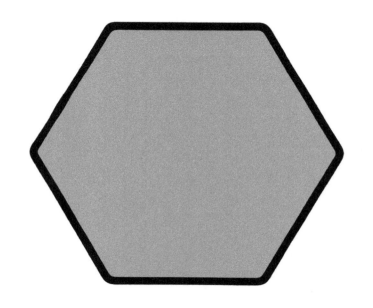

Sechseck

Sex-eck

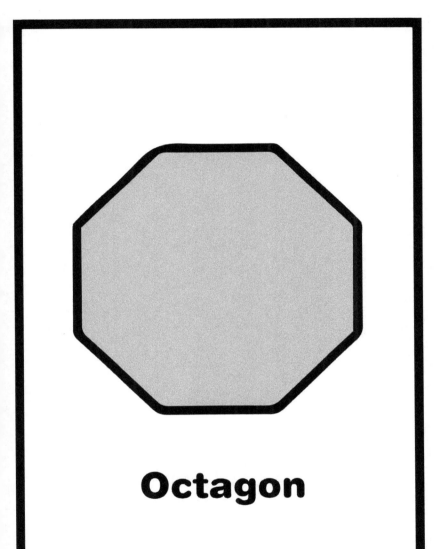

Octagon

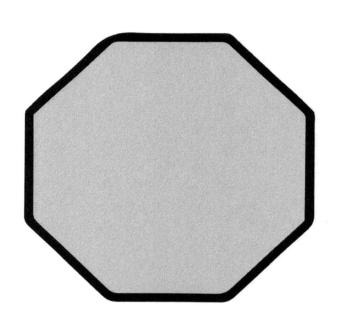

Achteck

Acht-eck

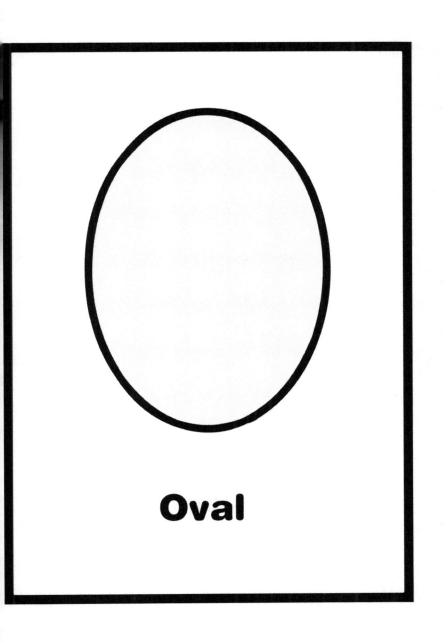

Oval

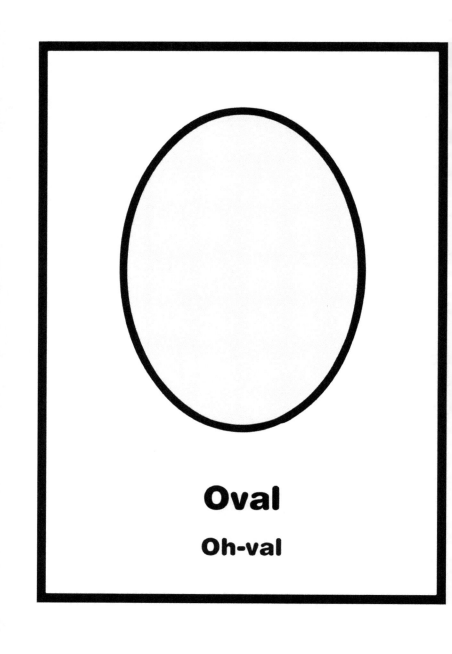

Oval

Oh-val

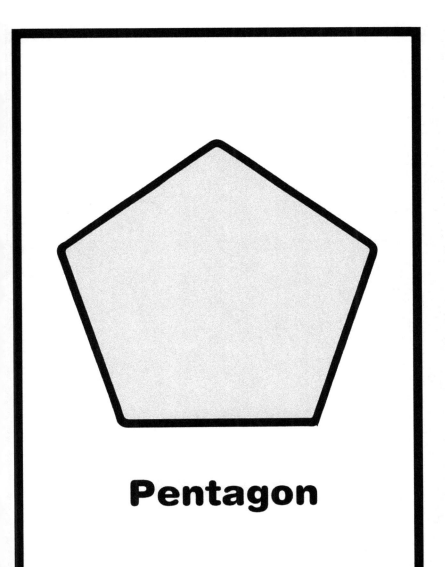

Pentagon

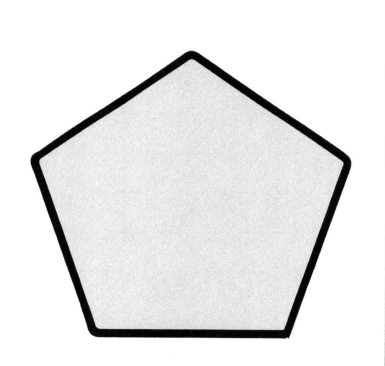

Fünfeck

Fue-nf-eck

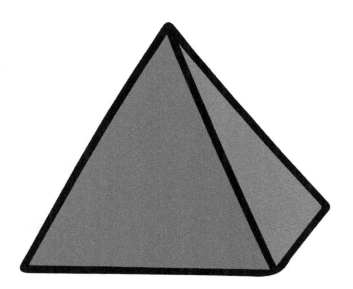

Pyramid

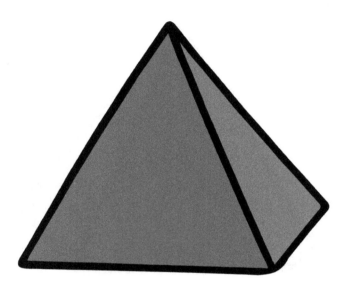

Pyramide

Pyra-me-deh

Rectangle

Rechteck

Recht-eck

Square

Viereck

Fear-eck

Star

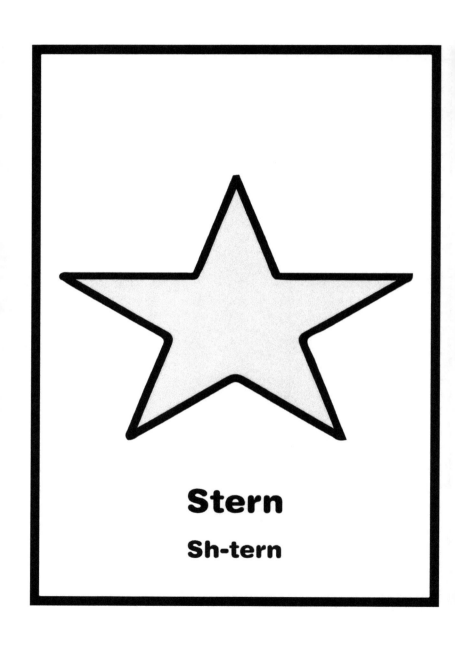

Stern

Sh-tern

Triangle

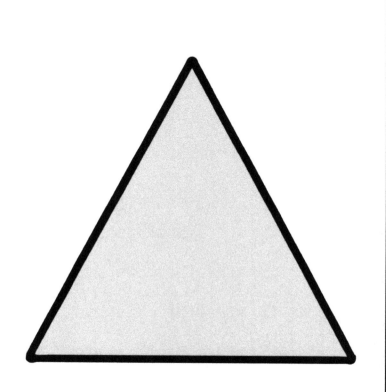

Dreieck

Dry-eck

Black

Schwarz

Sh-wards

Blue

Blau

Blau

Brown

Braun

Brown

Green

Grün

Gruen

Pink

Pink

Pink

Purple

Lila

Li-la

Red

Rot

Ro-t

White

Weiß

Why-ss

Yellow

Gelb

Gelb

Grey

Das Grau

Grau